THE TIVERTON MUSEUM RAILWAY COLLECTION

Compiled by Amyas Crump

ISBN 978-1-906419-39-4

First published in 2010 by Kevin Robertson under the **NOODLE BOOKS** imprint
PO Box 279 Corhampton, SOUTHAMPTON SO32 3ZX

www.kevinrobertsonbooks.co.uk

Printed in England by The Information Press.

PUBLISHERS NOTE

The origins of this book are unusual to say the least and consequently worthy of brief explanation. 125 plus years ago, W J Cotton was a Civil Engineer working on the construction of what came to be the Exe Valley railway from Stoke Canon to Tiverton.

To assist in his work he maintained records in a pocket notebook, part textual and part illustrative, the latter superb colour-wash drawings of a number of the important structures on the line. No doubt other men in similar position did likewise, although such notebooks rarely appear to have survived.

Subsequent to his work in the Exe Valley, Mr Cotton disappears from note. His later whereabouts, career history and indeed life are unknown of, that is until 1993 when his notebook surfaced as part of a collection of books found on sale in Freemantle, Australia. Through the kindness of several individuals, this valuable, possibly even unique artefact was repatriated and now reposes in the Museum at Tiverton.

Its existence was mentioned in conversation between Amyas Crump and myself in early 2009, although at the time purely as a conversation point.

Add to this notebook, a selection of contemporary images and plans, plus material drawn from the archives of The Broad Gauge Society and other private collections and the result is a wonderful record of railway planning and construction in the Victorian era. As the Museum also holds material relative to the nearby Culm Valley Railway, it makes sense also to include contemporary material from this route as well.

This book is not intended to be a complete facsimile reproduction of Mr Cotton's notes, to do so would be both repetitious and impractical, instead we are proud to present examples of some of the best material there is both from the notebook and other relevant railway items.

None of this material could be brought to a wider audience without the assistance of Amyas Crump, Tiverton Museum and of course The Broad Gauge Society. To them all I owe a debt of gratitude.

Kevin Robertson

SETTING THE SCENE

The first railway to reach Tiverton, was the Bristol and Exeter company's Tiverton Branch from Tiverton Road (later Tiverton Juntion), in June 1848 and built to the broad gauge. This was followed, in August 1884, by the opening of a line from the north, running from a junction with the Taunton - Barnstaple route east of Dulverton, south to Tiverton by way of Bampton. In 1884 the original line was converted to the standard gauge. In anticipation of this, the 1884 'Tiverton and North Devon Railway' and later 'Exe Valley Railway', arriving from the south, were constructed to the standard gauge from the outset. The latter line, from a junction at Stoke Canon, opened in May 1885. All three lines survived into British Railways days, although the north - south link was closed in 1963 and the original branch from Tiverton Junction the following year. Had the promoter's original plans come to fruition, the line south could have been extended to join the LSWR near Crediton or the Bristol and Exeter north of Stoke Canon at Rewe. The original Tiverton Branch had been built to allow for double track: in anticipation of an extension to Barnstaple and Bideford along a similar route to that later used by the Devon & Somerset and Tiverton & North Devon lines. Seen above is the earliest known railway view from the area, taken at Tiverton with a wonderful array of station staff. Recorded in broad-gauge days, it shows B & E Rly. No 58, later GWR No 2056, new in October 1859, which remained in service until November 1880.

The Broad Gauge Society

TO BUILD A RAILWAY

Having aroused interest within the local community and attracted the attention of potential investors, the next step was to attempt a Parliamentary Bill authorising construction.

It was at this stage that numerous schemes floundered, although that relating to the Tiverton area was of course ultimately successful.

In support of the proposal would be volumes of correspondence and countless maps, a general area illustration relative to the proposal is seen opposite. This would be followed by the Deposited Plans and Sections: an example of which is recorded on pages 6 – 9.

Certainly unusually, perhaps even almost uniquely, those that survive for the Tiverton and North Devon Railway, include reference marks made by the engineer indicating various bench or datum points used.

The Engineer in Charge of construction of the Tiverton and North Devon Railway was reported as H C Sanders, seen here. (There is also a reference to Mr Francis Fox having held the position in March 1884.) It is unlikely this was the company transport: a pony and trap appears in another view. Mr Cotton would have worked under him.   Tiverton Museum

TIVERTON & NORTH DEVON RAILWAY.

Plans and Sections.

TO BUILD A RAILWAY

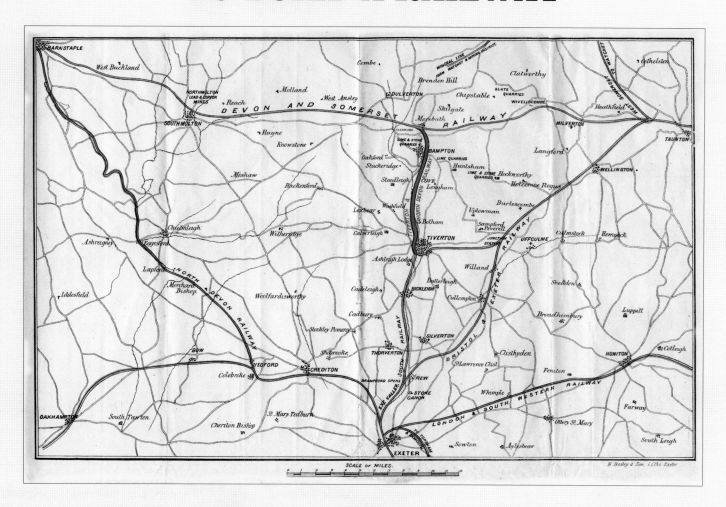

"...a Railway from a Junction with the Exe Valley South (Extension) Railway of the Bristol and Exeter Railway at Tiverton to the Town of Bampton, and thence to Morbath, there joining the Devon and Somerset Railway…"

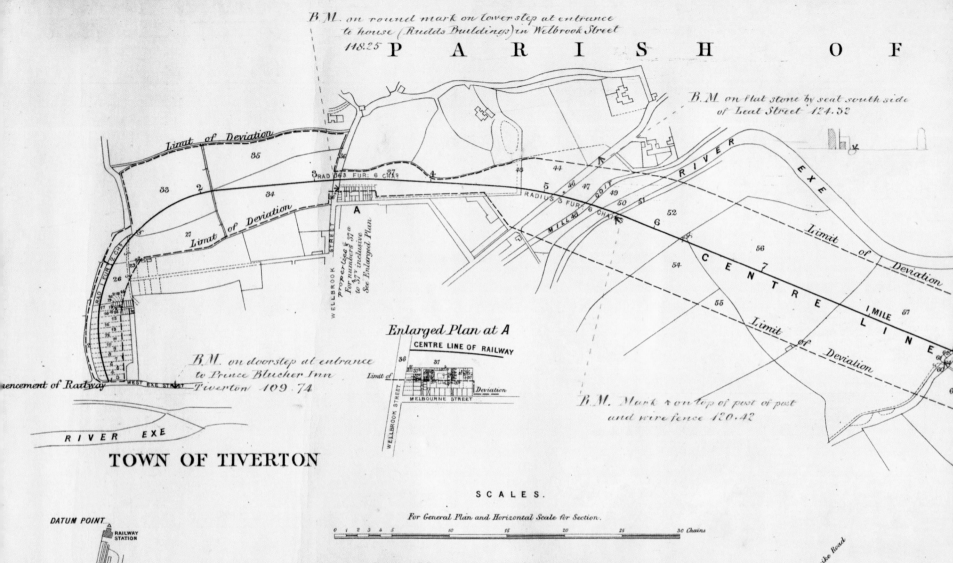

B.M. on round mark on lower step at entrance
to house (Rudds Buildings) in Welbrook Street
118.25

B.M. on flat stone by seat south side
of Leat Street 124.52

Limit of Deviation

35

33   2   34

3 RAD 663 FUR: 6 CHNS   4   44   46   47   49   50   51   52   56   57

RADIUS 3 FUR: 6 CHAINS   6   55   54

27   A

Limit of Deviation

26

MILL 45   6 OIT

RIVER   EXE   CENTRE   LINE

1 MILE

Limit   of   Deviation

Limit   of   Deviation

WELLBROOK STREET

Properties &
For numbers 37ᵃ
to 37ᵗ inclusive
See Enlarged Plan

WEST EXE STREET

B.M. on doorstep at entrance
to Prince Blucher Inn
Tiverton 109.74

mencement of Railway

Enlarged Plan at A

CENTRE LINE OF RAILWAY

36   37

Limit of   Deviation

WELLBROOK STREET

MELBOURNE STREET

B.M. Mark + on top of post of post
and wire fence 120.42

RIVER   EXE

TOWN OF TIVERTON

DATUM POINT

RAILWAY
STATION

GAS
WORKS

SCALES.

For General Plan and Horizontal Scale for Section.

0 1 2 3 4 5   10   15   20   25   30 Chains

For enlarged Plans and Horizontal Scale for accompanying Sections.

0 1 2 3 4 5   10   15 Chains

Horizontal Scale for Cross Sections of Roads.

0 1 2 3 4 5   10   15   20 Chains

Vertical Scale for General Section.

0 10 20 30 40 50   100   150   200   250   300   350   400 Feet

Vertical Scale for Cross Sections of Roads.

0 10 20 30 40 50   100   150   200 Feet

Turnpike Road

1 IN 66

100 feet above datum

Section at A to the same horizontal scale

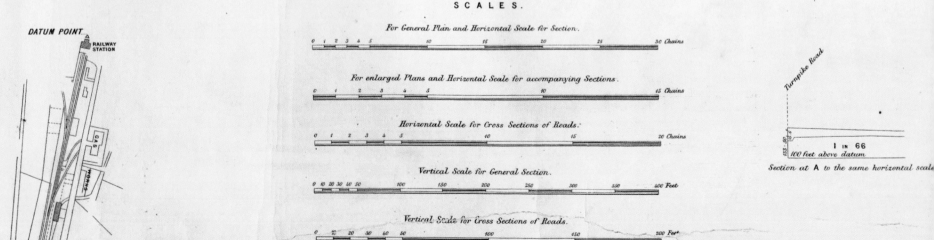

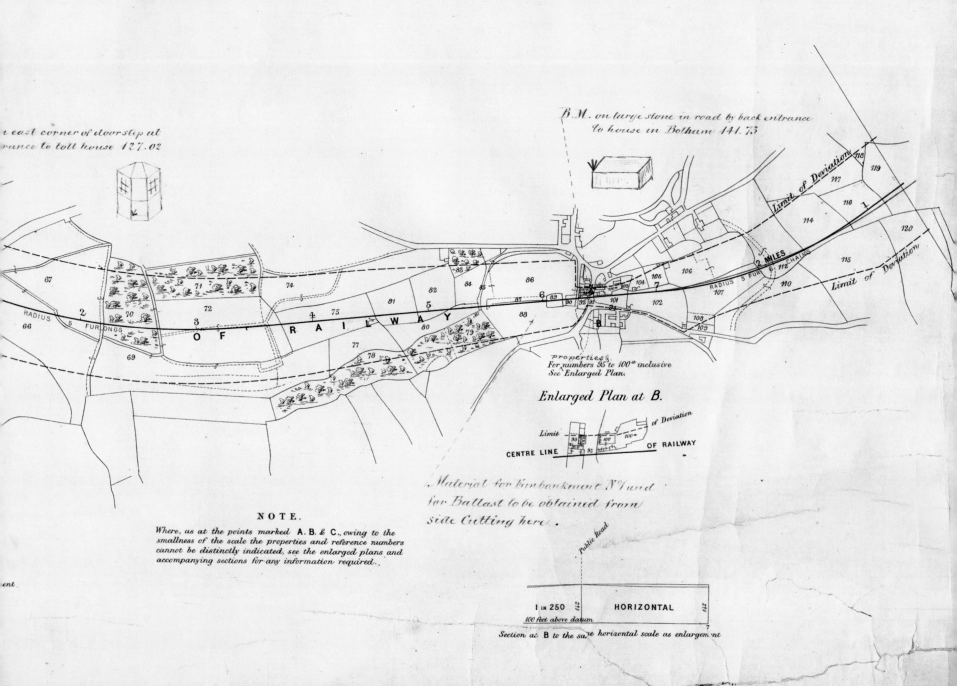

TIVERTON

east corner of doorstep at
rance to toll house 127.02

B.M. on large stone in road by back entrance
to house in Bolham 141.73

Limit of Deviation

Limit of Deviation

Limit of Deviation

2 MILES

RADIUS 3 FUR. 6. CHAINS

RADIUS 5 FURLONGS

OF RAILWAY

properties.
For numbers 95 to 100ᵃ inclusive
See Enlarged Plan.

Enlarged Plan at B.

Limit   of Deviation

CENTRE LINE   OF RAILWAY

Material for Embankment Nº 7 and
for Ballast to be obtained from
side Cutting here.

NOTE.

Where, as at the points marked A.B.& C., owing to the
smallness of the scale the properties and reference numbers
cannot be distinctly indicated, see the enlarged plans and
accompanying sections for any information required.

Public Road

1 IN 250   HORIZONTAL

100 feet above datum

Section at B to the same horizontal scale as enlargement.

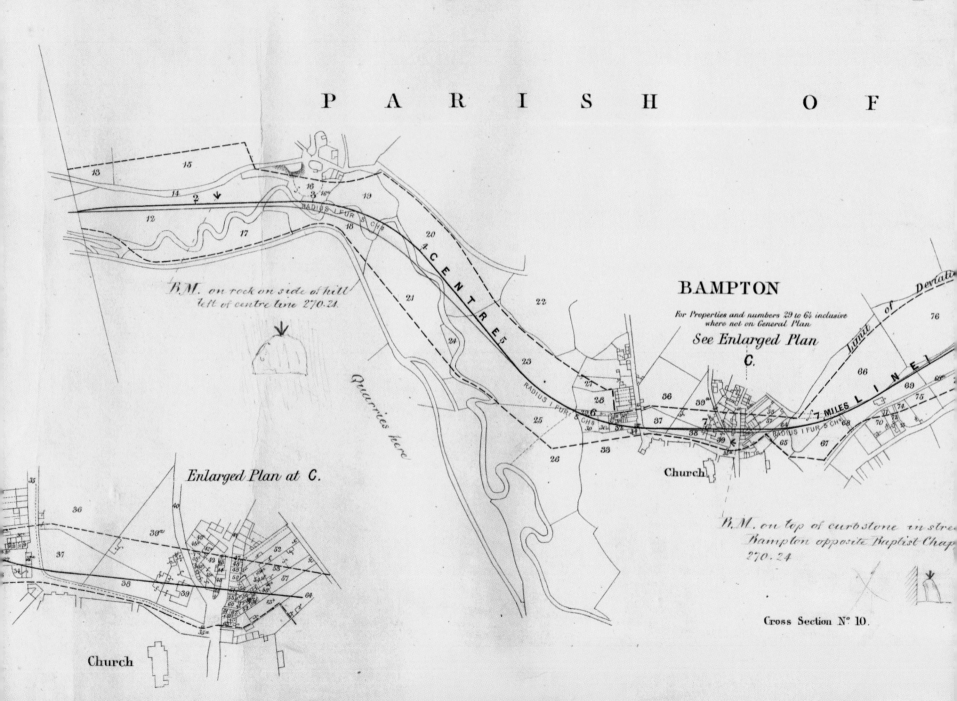

BAMPTON

For Properties and numbers 29 to 64 inclusive
where not on General Plan

See Enlarged Plan
C.

B.M. on rock on side of hill
left of centre line 270.24.

Quarries here

RADIUS 1 FUR 5 CHS

CENTRE

RADIUS 1 FUR 5 CHS

7 MILES LINE

Limit of Deviation

RADIUS 1 FUR 5 CHS

Church

B.M. on top of curbstone in street
Bampton opposite Baptist Chapel
270.24

Enlarged Plan at C.

Church

Cross Section Nº 10.

DEVON

BAMPTON

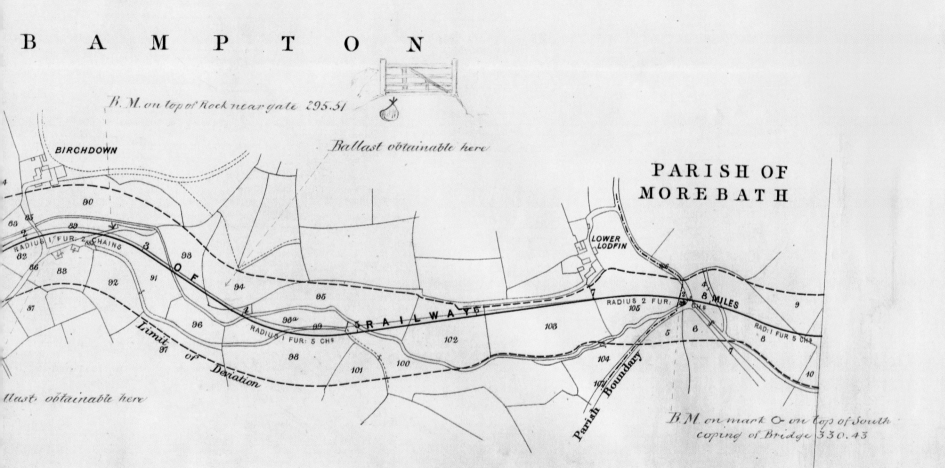

B.M. on top of Rock near gate 295.51

Ballast obtainable here

BIRCHDOWN

PARISH OF MORE BATH

90

88 85

2
RADIUS 1 FUR: 2 CHAINS
82

86   88

92   91

87

Limit of Deviation

Ballast obtainable here

O F

94

3

95

96

98

4

98a

RADIUS 1 FUR: 5 CHS

99

101

100

102

103

R A I L W A Y

LOWER
LODFIN

108

104

Parish Boundary

RADIUS 2 FUR:
105

8 MILES

4
CHS

5   6

RAD: 1 FUR 5 CHS

9

10

B.M. on mark ⊙ on top of South
coping of Bridge 330.43

AN ENGINEER'S NOTES

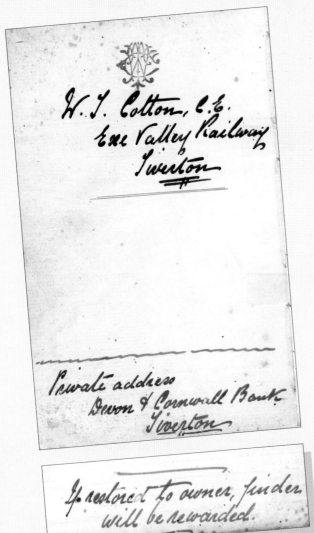

W. J. Cotton, C.E.

Exe Valley Railway

Tiverton

Private address
Devon & Cornwall Bank
Tiverton

If restored to owner, finder will be rewarded.

TIVERTON STATION.

Contractor William Veals. Bristol.

Total amount of Contract 5880.0.0

Schedule of Prices

Completion Price			£.s.d
1.6	Excavation	Cyd	1.3
.3	Filling	"	.4
9.6	Concrete	"	7.0
7.0	Masonry Fitted Rubble	"	15.0
13.0	" Random "	"	10.0
14.0	" Ashlar	"	16.0
1.3.0	Brickwork in Mortar	"	19.6
1.8.0	" " Cement	"	1.4.0
4.0	Bath Stone dressed work of all kinds	Cft	2.10
6.0	Pennant Stone plain	"	5.0
	" " landing	"	10.0
	" " Steps	"	6.9
4.6	Doulting Stone dressed work of all kinds	"	3.6
	Paving of 10"x5"x2" blue chequered		
3.3	" " tiles laid	Suyrd	3.6
	Ditto in coping as specified	Ydrun	5.0
4.0	Asphalte for paving Conv. tar	Suyrd	2.0
	Ditto	"	6.0
3.0	Damp Proof Course "3 Courses"	"	4.6
	1½" Punched Pennant Hearthstone	Suyft	
1.9	fixed Complete	Suyft	1.0
1.9	1½" Ditto do to	"	1.6
1.7	1¼" Sawn Slate Paving Cement jointed	"	1.2
1.0.0	Plane Slate Chimney pieces tubbed oiled and fixed	each	1.10.0
1.15.0	Enamelled ditto fixed	"	2.5.0
2.15.0	Marble do do do	"	4.0.0
1.19.6	Countess Close Slating on bottom	Upper Square	1.17.0
1.19.6	Duchess do " do nailed	"	2.0.0

Left - The inside (and inside rear) pages of Mr Cotton's notebook. At first glance little more than a well worn pocket book measuring just 6 inches x 3 inches. Its contents however reveal a treasure trove of material: a glimpse back into the working mind of the Victorian surveyor and engineer.

Above and right - Specification and plan for the new station at Tiverton. Notice 1st, 2nd and 3rd class Waiting Rooms.

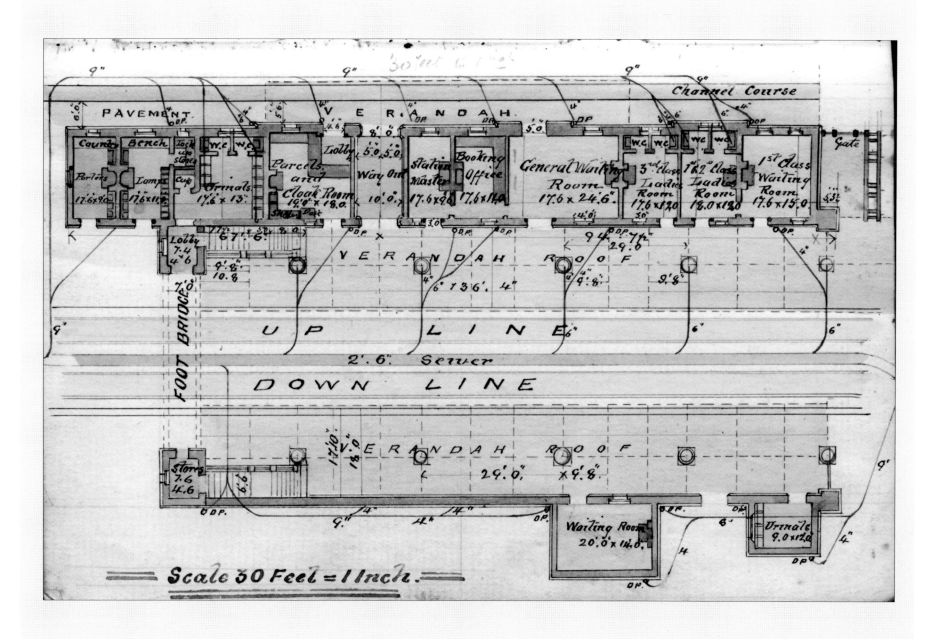

Scale 30 Feet = 1 Inch.

IRON GIRDER BRIDGE.

M.C. 10 5¾   Over West Exe Street Tiverton.

Skew.   12°

Height above road to underside of girders, 15'.0"

Width between abutments.   30'.0"

Masonry total fitted Rubble 261 C yd.
19/- pr Cubic Yard   Total £ 247.9.0
Coping
Total amount returned in bolts & nuts   Ton 2.0.17
Total Amount of Iron returned in final 13.17.1.0

Ironwork Detail

Flange.
Web
Gusset   } Tons. Cwt Qrs Ills.
Other plates &   } 3 . 16. 3. 3.
Flange plates round curved edges

Angle irons 3" x 3" x ⅜"
Stiffeners   2½" x 2½" x ⅜"   } 2 . 6 . 1 . 10.
&   2" x 1½" x ¼"

Cross Girders 12.   } 2 . 16 . 0 . 9.
Angle irons 2½" x 2½" x ⅜" } 2 . 8 . 2 . 7.
Diagonal Bracing 2½" x 2½" x ⅜"   . 6 . 0 . 9.

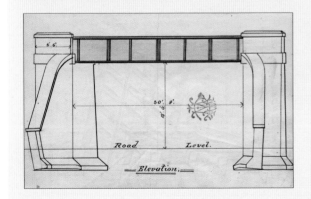

Elevation.

---

6 M. 79 Chs.

Materials.		RATE	£	s.	d.
Brickwork in Mortar					
including Invert	65 C yds	2q	65	0	0
Cast Iron					
	Tons 1.10.0.0	9/-	13	10	0
Wrot Iron					
	Tons 2.1.1.15	14/-	33	0	6
Wrot Iron in bolts &c.					
	Tons	24/-			
Creosoted Timber	73 qr	3/-			
Stone Pitching 6"	32.	2/6	4	0	0
Excavation					
Total cost about			115	10	6

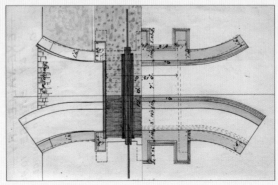

FLY BRIDGE AT ST ANDREWS ST. 10 M. 14¾ C.

From Rail Level to Soffit of Arch 14.3"

From Rail Level to Road Level   17.0"

Span on square   24.9"

Rise of Arch   5.0

Skew of Bridge   17°

This Fly Bridge has had to give place to a Brick abutment Bridge, owing to the continual slipping of the Cutting, rendering it impossible to get in the footings.

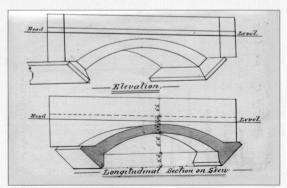

Road   Level.
Elevation.
Road   Level.
Longitudinal Section on Skew

BRIDGES AND CULVERTS

CATTLE ARCH & INVERT AT 6 M. 79 Chs.

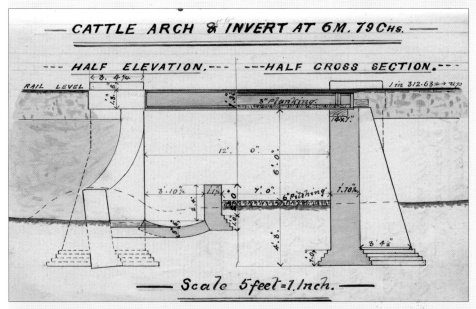

HALF ELEVATION.

HALF CROSS SECTION.

RAIL LEVEL

1 in 312.63 ꝯ up

3" Planking

14×7"

12'. 0"

6'. 0"

6" pitching

7'. 10½"

3'. 10½"

3'. 4½"

4'. 8"

Scale 5 feet = 1 Inch.

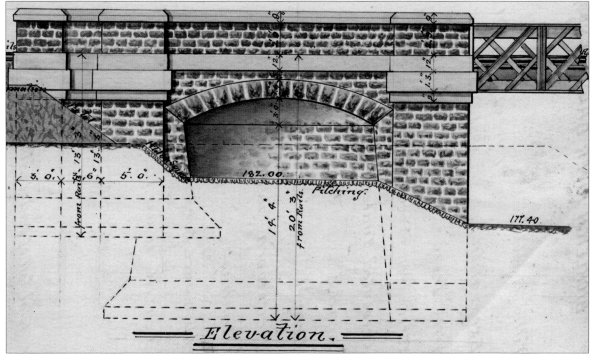

182.00.

Pitching.

177.40

Elevation.

IRON GIRDER BRIDGE AT 6 M. 79 Chs.
IRON BRIDGE WITH STONE FLOOD OPENINGS.

Iron Girder Bridge built over the River Exe
at Bickleigh, with one Stone Flood Opening
at each end. Bridge is built on
a Curve of 50 Chain Radius, and at an
Angle of 45°.
Three spans of 50 ft in clear, or square.

CATTLE ARCH & INVERT AT 6 M 79 Chs.

Brick Cattle Arch at 6.79.
Span 12 ft. Invert 5 ft
Headway 6 ft.

Creosoted Timber

Brickwork in Mortar   65 c yd @ 20/- 65.0.0

Wrot Ironwork

Cast Ironwork

Cost of Brick Invert.

	Rate	£	s	d
Brickwork in Mortar	to c yd			
Excavation				
Total about £				

BRIDGES AND CULVERTS

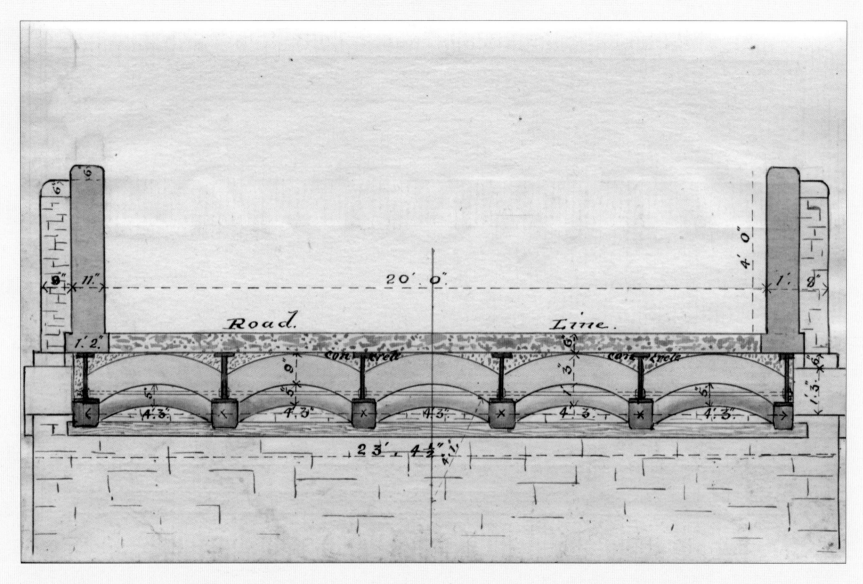

A final example of one of the magnificent bridge drawings from the notebook. Curiously, despite copious notes appearing opposite every other example, the location of this particular girder bridge was not quoted. (Either West Exe Street or a proposal for St Andrews Street perhaps?)

CROSSING COTTAGE

Aside from the structures necessary for the railway, Mr Cotton also recorded some - but not all of the buildings along the route. This is the crossing keepers cottage at Cove between Tiverton and Bampton and where a siding had also been provided from the outset - the rational for which was to attract goods traffic from nearby quarries.

Although from the plans seen as primitive by modern day standards, the cottage was substantially built. (See page 42.)

In 1923 a formal passenger Halt was established at Cove which survived until the line's closure. Its 'Pagoda' shelter now serves Donniford Halt on the nearby West Somerset Railway.

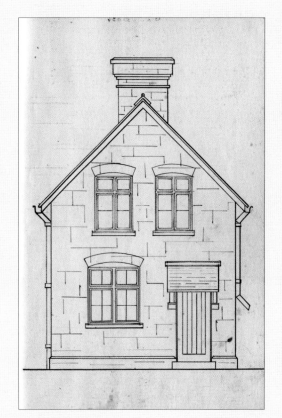

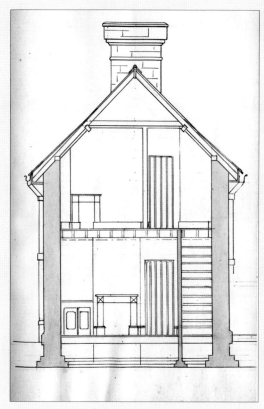

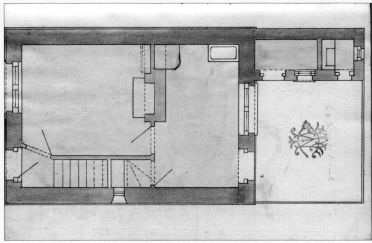

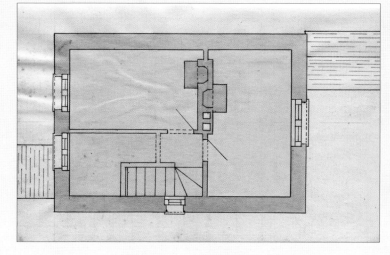

A postcard view of the 'New' Tiverton station looking south towards Cadeleigh and eventually Stoke Canon. Although postmarked 20 February 1906, it is likely the scene is much earlier, possibly even dating from very close to the mid 1880s opening time: as witness the inside-keyed track. The starting signal can be seen to be of the slotted-post type, unusually with scalloped paint at the base of the post. One concession towards modernity is that the ballast does not totally cover the top of the sleepers. To the left is a standard GWR Engineering Department wheelbarrow and a painter appears still to be at work on the fence. Although in later years the station was famed for its enamel signs, in this view the name appears simply painted on. To the right is the stock of the 'Tivvy Bumper'. Later track alterations provided for a bay on the left, to avoid the Bumper having to cross the Exe Valley lines. In the distance is the original signal box. Wagons are being attended to in the Down platform whilst a train from Exeter approaches.

CONSTRUCTION

Two views from February and March 1883 at Tiverton. Work has started and the foundations are well under way with various temporary buildings erected. The contractor for the Exe Valley section was Wm. Moss, who later settled in Thorverton. A number of his branded scaffold planks, like those shown here, survive today as the floor of a local barn.

A month later and the Up side building is progressing (see Page 11). Wooden scaffolding is being erected using ropes: a far cry from today. Across the yard can be seen the paling fence and nameboard of the platform of the B & E station, and a little to the right the signal box. To the right of both views is the extended goods shed. Sadly none of the broad gauge stock and what may be a locomotive to the left of the signal box, are clear enough for proper identification.

A ceremonial spade, used to turn the first sod in the new works reposes in Tiverton Museum.

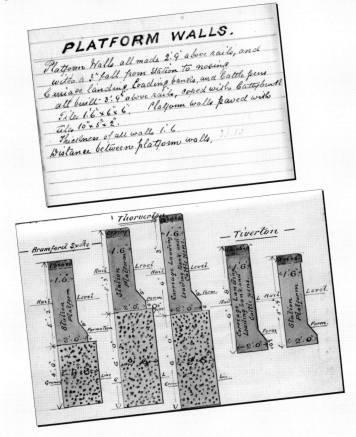

This page - North of Tiverton, the contractor was Nathaniel B Fogg of Liverpool, at Bampton the station and goods shed are seen, the latter constructed before the rails actually reached the station. The constructional views in this series were taken by Mr Sanders and repose in the care of Tiverton Museum. Bampton was similar to, but not the same as the Exe Valley stations, the latter more alike. Although not referred to in the notebook, part of the delay in construction south of Bampton was a local solicitor, Mr Loosemore. He was a landowner in his own right but objected very strongly to the railway. As the alignment across his land was fenced off and earthworks commenced, so he employed men to put it all back at night! Such difficulties were rare, but not unknown elsewhere in the country. Eventually with the help of Police Constables and Magistrates order was restored.

Opposite page - The T & ND surveyor noted 'Quarries' (pages 8/9), to the rear of this scene. A siding extended from behind the goods shed into the quarry, which had its own internal narrow gauge railway system. Even by the early 1920s, Messrs Scotts were using a fleet of Sentinel steam lorries rather than rail to deliver their roadstone.

BAMPTON STATION.

Contractors, Messrs Stephens & Bastow
Builders   Bristol

Contract signed July 17th 1882.

Amount of Contract £1848. 0. 0.

Schedule of Price as pr list on left side of Tiverton Schedule already given

Particulars of Specification regarding material, workmanship &c almost identical with Tiverton as given

MR COTTON'S RECORD

"The Exe Valley Railway commences at a junction with the GW Rly at a point about 15 chains below the present Stoke Canon Station and 4 miles above St Davids Station Exeter. It is a light railway with a simple road running to Tiverton, there joining the Tiverton & North Devon Rly which runs to Bampton and forms a junction with the Devon & Somerset line to Barnstaple and Ilfracombe. At Stoke the junction is made with a double road which continues for about 13 chains and there runs into a simple road.

A broad gauge also runs to 0.23 and then terminates. No 1 cutting commences almost at the junction and runs out in about 20 chains, average depth 4 feet, total quantity, 2,800 cu.yds.

The line starts on a gradient of 1 in 300 up and on a curve of 15 chains to 0.26 when a reverse curve of 30 chains runs to 0.44. At 0.23, 0.35, 0.44 and 0.56 are flood openings with 1, 2 & 3 openings of 10 feet span and 6 feet headway which it was found necessary to construct to provide for the heavy floods which at times come down the valley. Making due allowance for floods caused considerable problems. On occasions the entire valley being under water for days.

After leaving No 1 cutting the road gets on to a bank of about an average depth of 4 feet to Brampford Speke Station which is situated at 0m 63 chains. This is on a gradient of 1 in 1000 which commences at 0.23½ and ends at 0.66 and on a curve of 30 chains which commences at 0.54 between which place and 0.44 there is a straight.

Brampford Speke Station is a building similar to the other stations on the Exe Valley Rly, it contains General and Ladies Waiting Rooms, Booking Office and Parcels Office. At the back of the building there is the Coal and Wood place, the Lamps and the Stores rooms. The building is of Westleigh stone, Ham Hill dressing and varnished Pitch pine wood work.

There is also provided for the Station Master a Cottage containing 3 bedrooms, parlour and Kitchen, yard pump and all Conveniences. Together with all the other new Stations and Cottages these were built by Mr Berry of Crediton, Devon.

At Brampford there is but the simple road and one platform. The village is reached by a footbridge over the Exe. Vehicles can only cross by fording the river which is only possible at times of low water. With one more flood opening at 0.74 we reach the first crossing of the River Exe which is done by an iron girder bridge of 3 spans each of 50 feet. The piers and abutments are built of Westleigh stone and the girders of wrought iron lattice work. Width of bridge 15 feet between the plates and 16 feet 9 inches from web to web. The total cost of this bridge is about £2,300. Stone pitching and a few piles were required to secure the river slopes.

From 0.54 to 1.9 there is a curve of 30 chains which runs over the iron bridge. After leaving the bridge the road runs over two brick cattle creeps one at 1.4½ one at 1.5¾ and on a bank of an average height of 4 feet to 1.20 when we come to Fortescue Level Crossing. A signal cabin is built here with 6 levers and a pair of folding gates worked by the wheel from the cabin. A cottage for the signalman has also been built which with the cost of maintenance makes a crossing far more expensive than a bridge. Mr May is the occupier of the farm at this place.

The gradient from 0.66 to 1.26 is 1 in 330 up. From 1.9 to 1.14 the line is straight and from 1.14 to 1.28 there is a curve of 21 chains radius. The line from Mr May's crossing at 1.21 runs almost on the ground level until it reaches 1.41 where there is a brick cattle creep. It then enters No 2 cutting, the largest cutting on the line. A total quantity of about 68,000 cu.yds of earth being taken from it. Its highest point is about 60 feet above formation. The old bed of the River Exe is plainly discernable in the cutting but at a height of about 85 feet above its present level. The thickness of the bed plainly revealed by gravel is about 25 feet. The ground at this place fell so rapidly that whilst on the west side the height was considerable, the east fell almost perpendicular to the water and to make the bank secure it was necessary to put in a considerable amount of stone on the river bank and fill with earth to about 8 feet from formation and finish with a random rubble wall to formation level, this is at 1.63. This cutting which commences at 1.42 ends at 2.1. A curve runs through the latter portion and a short reverse curve on entering it to get away a little further from the river.

From 1.28 to 1.44 straight, then a small curve for 5 chains. Then from 1.49 to 1.65 straight. From 1.65 to 1.75 is a curve 21 chains and from 1.75 to 2.1 is a straight.

The route from 1.26 to 1.32¼ is level, from 1.32¼ to 1.67 is 1 in 100 up. From 1.67 to 1.69 level and from 1.69 to 2.7¼ 1 in 100 down. Directly on emerging from the cutting there is a bank which runs to Thorverton at 2.50 of an average depth of 8 feet, one brick cattle creep at 2.15 and an occupation bridge at 2.43. At 2.50 there is a P.R. bridge under the line and this point is the beginning of the double road for the Thorverton Station.

The Station is at 2.55 and is similar to Brampford Speke but on the up platform there is a waiting shelter and there is also here a Goods Station and Goods Yard with a strong and commodious Goods Shed containing Crane, Office and skeleton lock-up.

At 2.60 there is a bridge under the line in passing which No 3 cutting is entered. This cutting has given considerable trouble being on the side of a steep field which gradually came away when the bottom or toe was cut away. It was remedied by raising the formation some 4 feet with rough ballast and piles being driven against the side of the cutting nearest the field, about 30 in number. In leaving the cutting the River Exe is again crossed by an iron girder bridge of the same class and style as Brampford Speke.

The gradient from 2.7¾ to 2.18 is level, from 2.18 to 2.50 1 in 132, from 2.50 to 2.63¾ and through Thorverton level. 2.6¾ to 3.1¼ 1 in 100 down, 3.1¼ to 3.20 1 in 60 up. From the river bridge at 3.3 to 3.7 there is a bank of an average height of 7 feet. At 3.7 a cattle creep with brick abutments and an iron trough girder top. At 3.27 Up Exe level crossing with signal box and a cottage, and at 3.36 Silverton Station *(- originally known as 'Up Exe and Silverton'. Later from 1 May 1905, the name 'Up Exe' was used.)* which is in all aspects like Brampford Speke with simple road and platform. A cottage is also built here for the Station Master. Another level crossing at 3.41 with signal box finishes Silverton.

3.20 to 3.41 is level and from 3.41 to 4.31 is 1 in 165 up. The road to 4.12 is about on the surface but at 4.12 No 5 cutting commences and ends at 5.23½. It is a long low cutting about 8 feet average depth. At 4.55 a brick fly arch is built over a public road and at 5.3 a stone bridge also for a public road. At 5.20 is situated Meme farm and from here to 6.40 is a long straight run. From 3.20 to 3.41 the road is level, from 3.41 to 4.31 1 in 165 up, from 4.31 to 4.50 level, from 4.50 to 5.00 1 in 2100 down, 5.0 to 5.19 level, 5.19 to 6.41 1 in 363.89 up and from 6.41 to 7.6 1 in 312.65 up.

At 6.41 there is a stream bridge with two openings and at 6.43 a Mill Stream with one opening. A curve of 40 chains radius runs into Bickleigh Station passing under a road bridge.

Bickleigh proved a very expensive place, about 8 bridges with a double 6 feet culvert besides smaller ones having to be built and the public road diverted for about 40 chains. A Goods Shed with Office, Waiting Shed, Cranes, Weighbridge and Office is also built here.

At 6.69 the River Exe is again crossed by an iron girder bridge similar to the two former. The line runs almost on the surface from here to near Ashleigh (now Ashley) at 9.6. At 8.40 the River Exe is so near the public road that difficulty was experienced in making room between them for the railway. The river had to be slightly diverted and a length of pitching for about 6 chains to protect the bank from the wash. A hoarding 3 feet high on the top of the Devonshire bank was put to separate the road from the railway. *(- this was to avoid complaints from horse owners.)*

At 8.63 another difficulty was encountered the room being so limited the sides of the bank were also pitched, and the sides of the cutting next the road, and a stone wall on top of the cutting between it and the road. Some land had to be taken from the west side to give proper width to the road but in cutting this away the side of the hill came down and caused much time, trouble and expense. A wall 6 feet thick was built for a short length which prevented further slipping. *(- see note page 24.)*

At 9.36, Ashleigh, the road had to be diverted and an expensive bridge with a culvert underneath built. At 9.70 a brick cattle arch, at 10.5 an iron girder bridge over West Exe Street Tiverton, at 10.7 a masonary bridge over Coombs Mill stream and a 10.10 a stone bridge with 4 openings over the River Exe. At 10.15 a brick bridge under St Andrews Street and at 10.18 an iron trough girder over the River Loman. At 10.27 a flood opening for same. Cutting from 10.28 to 10.46, 10.44 Cullompton fly bridge and at 10.48 Tiverton Station."

A coffer dam and temporary bridge over the River Exe, Thorverton, June 1883.

MR COTTON'S RECORD

Specification for laying Permanent Way and Contract Conditions

All materials and fittings handed over to the Contractor; he will be responsible for both the quantity and damage. Length 10m. 63ch., also loop at Stoke Canon and loops and sidings at Thorverton, Bickleigh (Cadeleigh), and Tiverton, with all necessary crossing work.

Ballast to be laid to line and level. Contractor to provide pegs and man, or men, to assist Engineer to set out or whatever required.

Great care is to be taken to lay the rails to true and regular lines, levels and curves, and with requisite cant and true gauge, line to be handed over in perfectly satisfactory state and with ballast placed in proper form as to width, thickness and level.

Contractor may use road but must take care.

Must make good all injuries to slopes or works through haulage or otherwise.

Sleepers to be laid square to rails, 1830 per mile. Chairs bolted to sleepers, evenly bedded, special chairs to river Bridges, double chairs to crossings.

Rails laid with usual expansion allowance, points fair and true, securely fished, exactly opposite in straight position, on curves 2¼" out of square only allowed.

Ballast to be opened out to the requisite extent. Permanent way properly packed with beaters (- a tool similar to a pick-axe with a 'T' shape end instead of a point: ideal for packing ballast) to 2½" above present level at 7" above ballast. Area left clear of packing of not less than 1½" top of sleepers generally level with ballast. Ballast neatly boxed up at sides and sloped off. 6 feet way to be as near height of rail as quantity will permit.

Great care to pack under outer part of sleepers and under rails.

Shale or inferior ballast to be left out, fresh supplied by contractor of line and deficiency made good. Contractor of permanent way must spread and pack and make good any falling down slopes.

All crossing work with its cuttings, connecting and fixing switches, crossings, buffer-stops to be performed at schedule of prices.

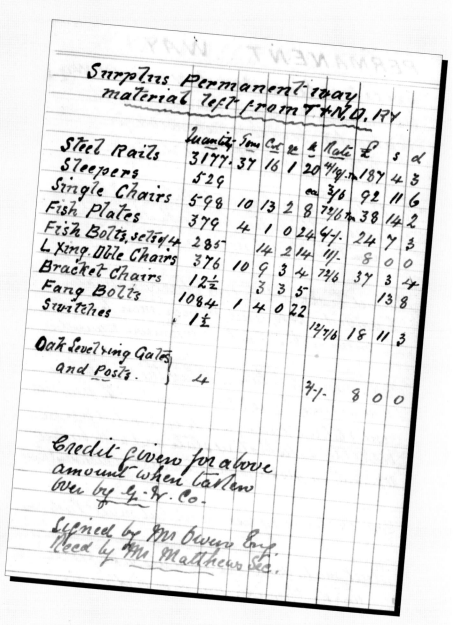

MR COTTON'S RECORD

Work to be completed to the satisfaction of the Engineer within 3 calendar months. If delayed in delivery this time not to count.

Contractor to be paid monthly 80 per-cent on work done, the remaining 20 per-cent to be paid two months after the opening of the line for traffic. Anything left unsatisfactory the Engineer at liberty to remedy it and deduct amount.

No Sunday work unless considered necessary by the Engineer.

No masonry pointing or other similar work shall be carried out in time of frost, and no work of any description shall be proceeded with when the weather is such as to remedy it liable to imperfections.

Precaution to be taken in carrying works across, over or under, paths, roads, canals and watercourses, to avoid injury or improperly interfering with traffic. Contractor liable for all injuries, damages or stoppages.

Railway passes granted to Contractor and principal agent, or assistant. To have been completed in 18 months: penalty £50 per week.

All extra works to be subjected to the same conditions, as the contract and payable at the same rates as the schedule of prices.

The whole of the work to be kept in perfect order and maintained by the contractor for 12 months after completion.

Advances to be made monthly on the Engineer's recommendation but 10% to be kept in hand.

Any disputes or differences to be settled by the Engineer, "that is between the Contractor and the Company".

March 1884.

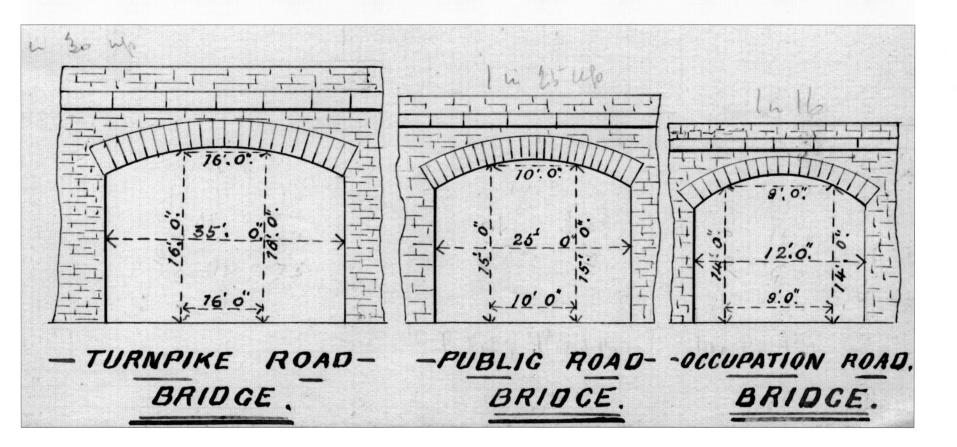

-TURNPIKE ROAD- BRIDGE.

-PUBLIC ROAD- BRIDGE.

-OCCUPATION ROAD. BRIDGE.

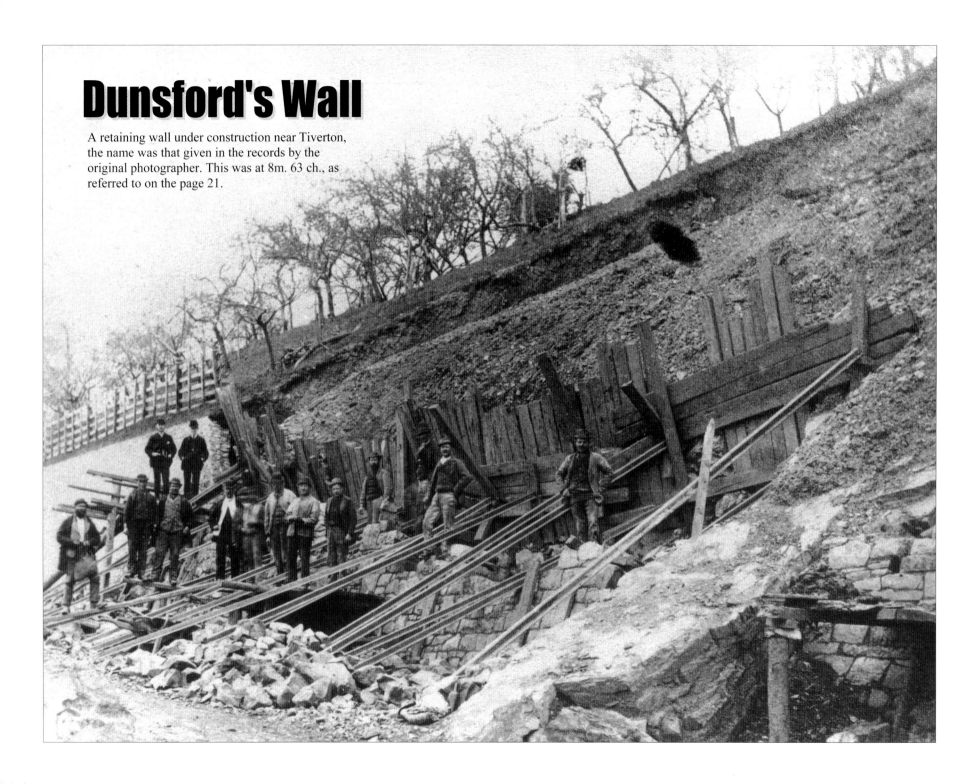

Dunsford's Wall

A retaining wall under construction near Tiverton, the name was that given in the records by the original photographer. This was at 8m. 63 ch., as referred to on the page 21.

Thorverton Bridge, July 1962.

The collapsed weir on the right provided a supply for Thorverton mill. Prior to building the line: the original mills blocking the alignment had been demolished and their leat diverted. The steam engines working on the construction site, page 21, are standing on a jetty where the group of cows are seen in this view. The dam was the site of the right hand pier.

J Strange / Amyas Crump collection

BROAD GAUGE AT TIVERTON

As previously recounted, the original railway to Tiverton was that from the junction station on the main line, at the appropriately named Tiverton Junction. Built to the broad gauge of 7 feet and a quarter inch, the station survived as the passenger terminus until the opening of the new Tiverton station in 1885: trains from Dulverton used this station until the opening of the new Tiverton station. Consequent upon the completion of the Exe Valley route, the terminus was relegated to a goods station.

No photographs of the original station appear to have survived, although it does appear in the background to several of the views in this book.

The remarkable plan seen here and overleaf, is the first true idea of the layout of the original facilities and has never been seen before. Drawn on linen and bound in leather, the plan is some six-feet in length, the work of a skilled surveyor and colour artist.

Worthy of detail study, one of principal items of note are the actual goods facilities: short sidings and

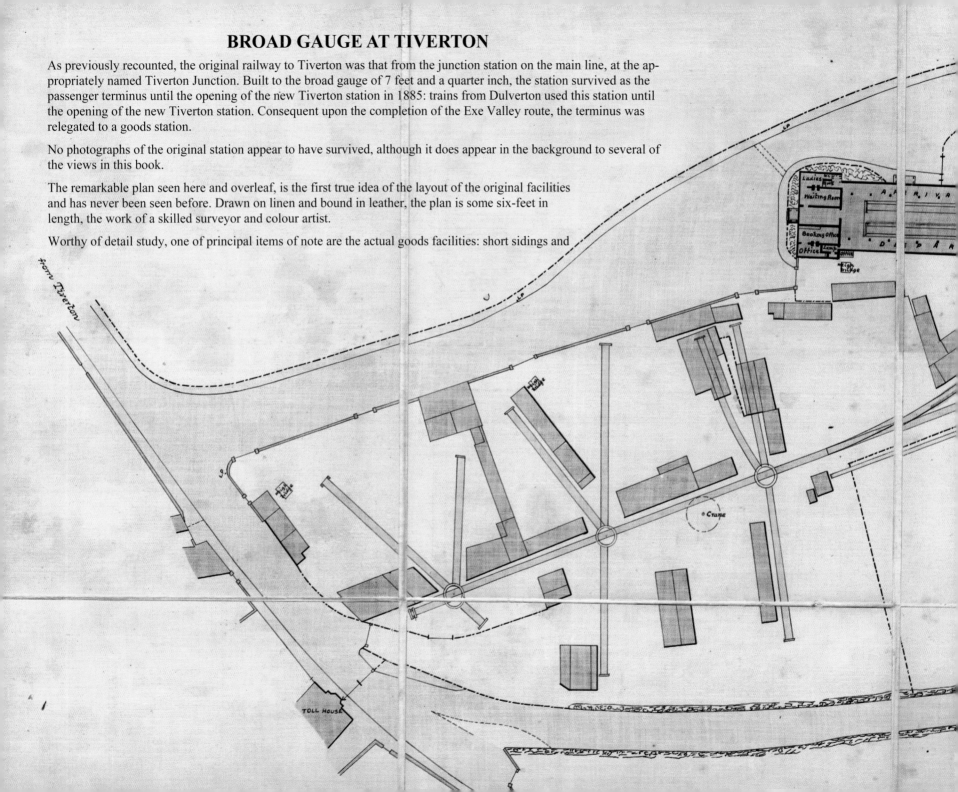

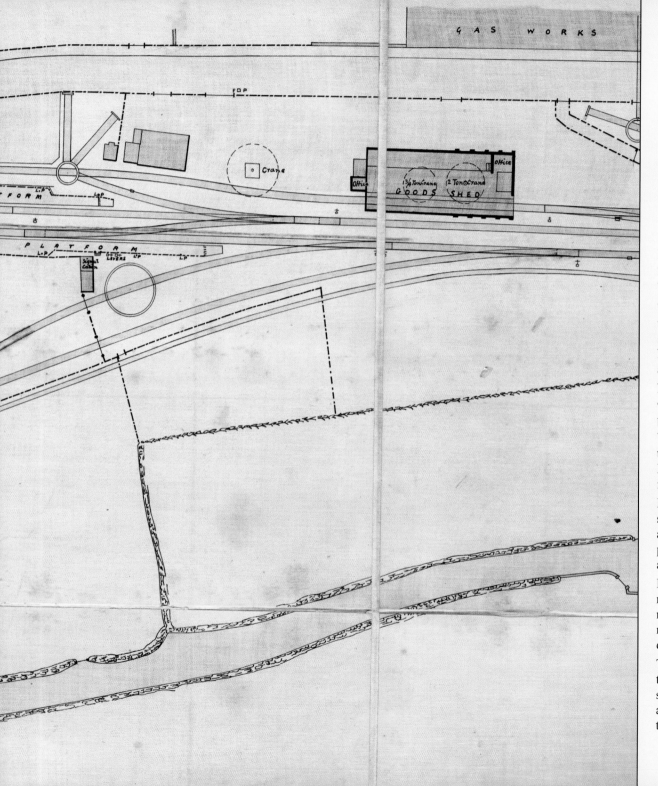

TIVERTON

hand operated wagon turntables, all indicative of the importance the early railways placed on goods traffic.

The site is shown at its peak in April 1884, at which time the branch was still broad gauge only, conversion not taking place until 29 June 1884. The T & ND Railway had been scheduled to open on 3 July, although this was delayed to 1 August.

Note the toll house and gate bottom left.

The road across the top was known as London Road before the building of the railway, then Station Road. With the opening of the new through station, the road to the Toll House became Station Road and the old London Road was renamed again, this time becoming Blundells Road.

Part of the Gas Works, with its rail entrance, still survives,, as does the sweeping curve of the road around the station, just opposite which is now a car park for Tesco. Sections of the coal yard walls can also still be seen.

In 1884, the only housing on the country side of the railway was Wilcombe Villas. The opening of the new station really opened up this area between the railway and canal basin, many villas displaying build dates of 1885 - 90.

Tiverton was enjoying an era of prosperity, importance and expansion at this time and the scale of the station facilities was commensurate with this. Unusually the station was only a few minutes walk from the town centre.

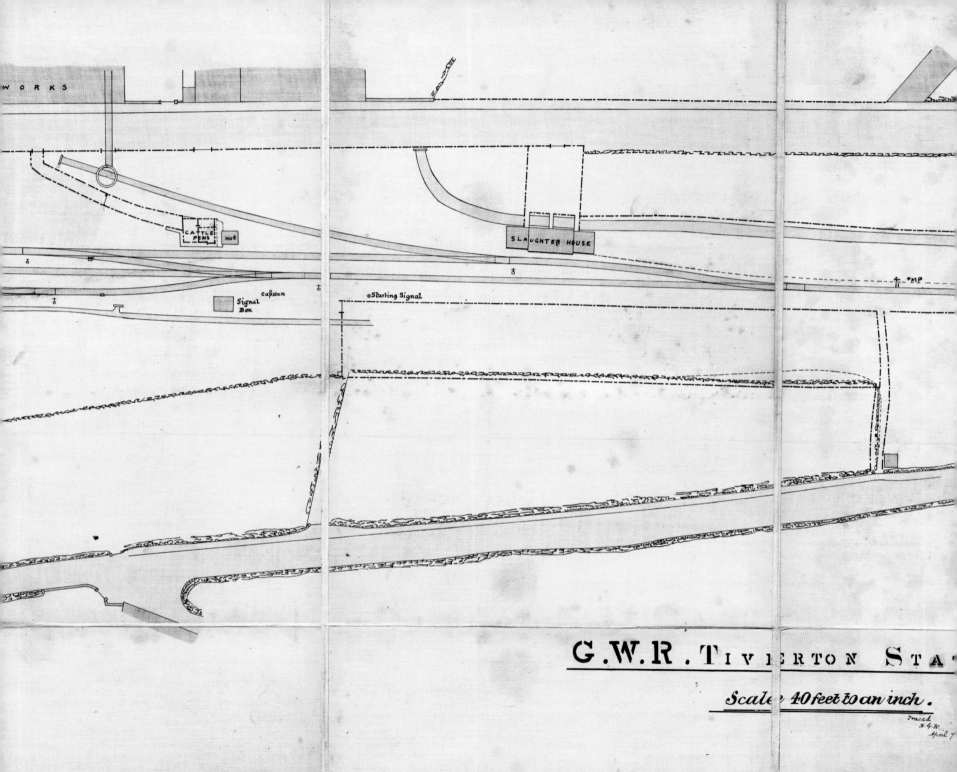

WORKS

CATTLE
PENS   Hut

SLAUGHTER HOUSE

Signal
Box

Capstan

Starting Signal

4 MP

G.W.R. TIVERTON STA

Scale 40 feet to an inch.

Traced
A.G.W.
April 7

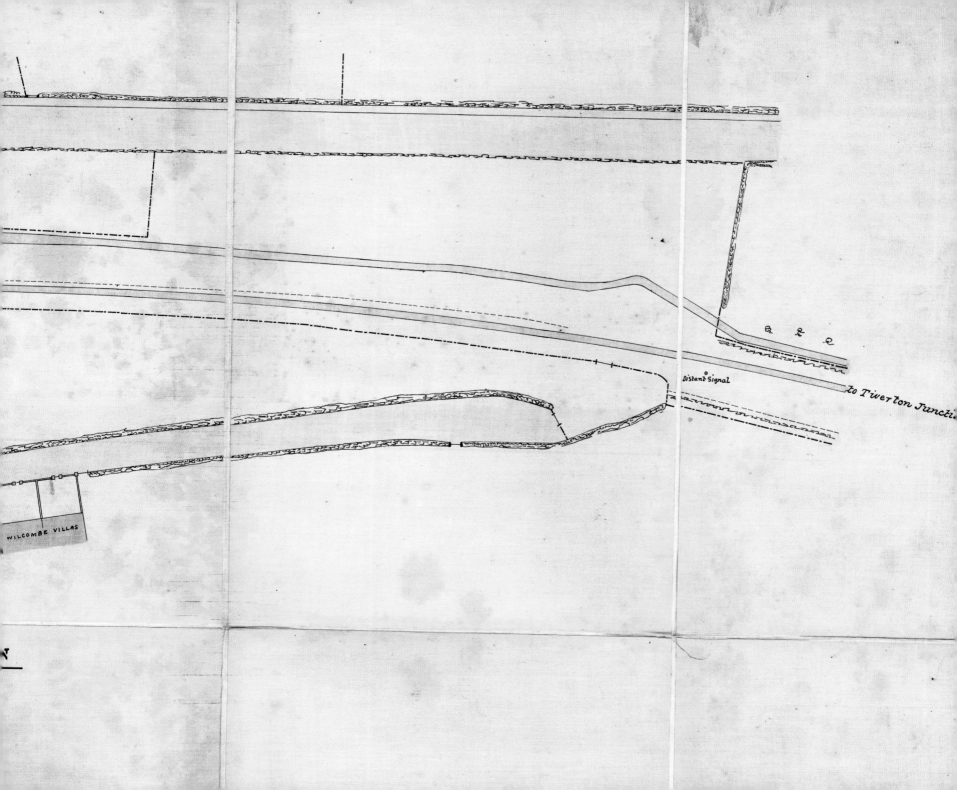

Distant Signal

to Tiverton Junction.

WILCOMBE VILLAS

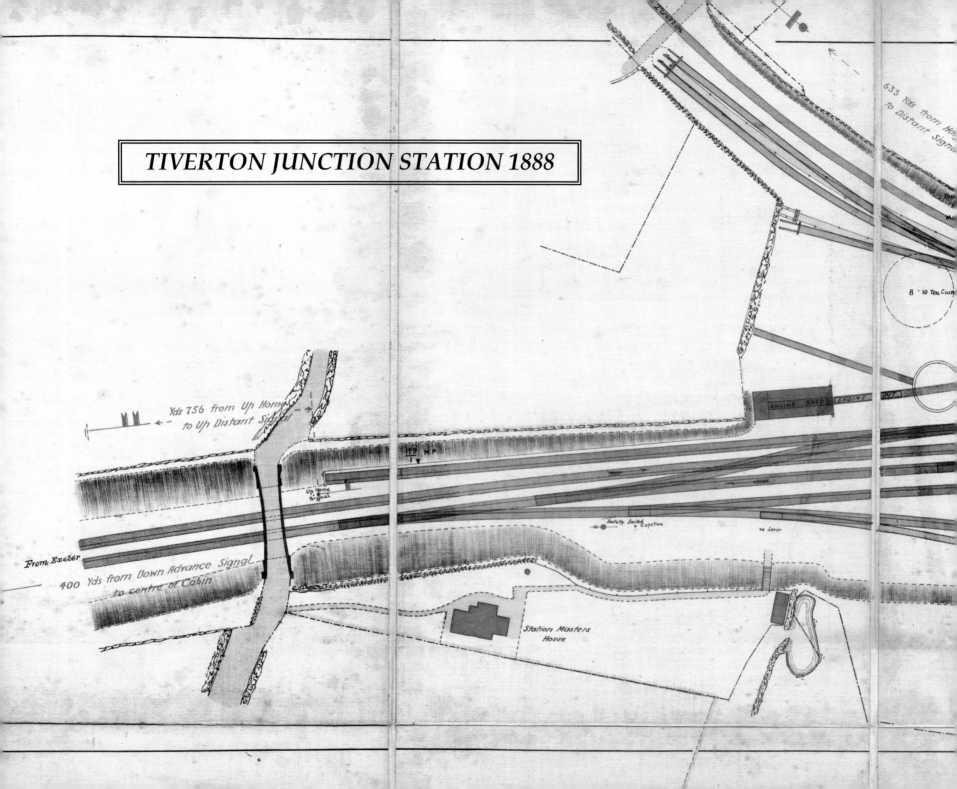

TIVERTON JUNCTION STATION 1888

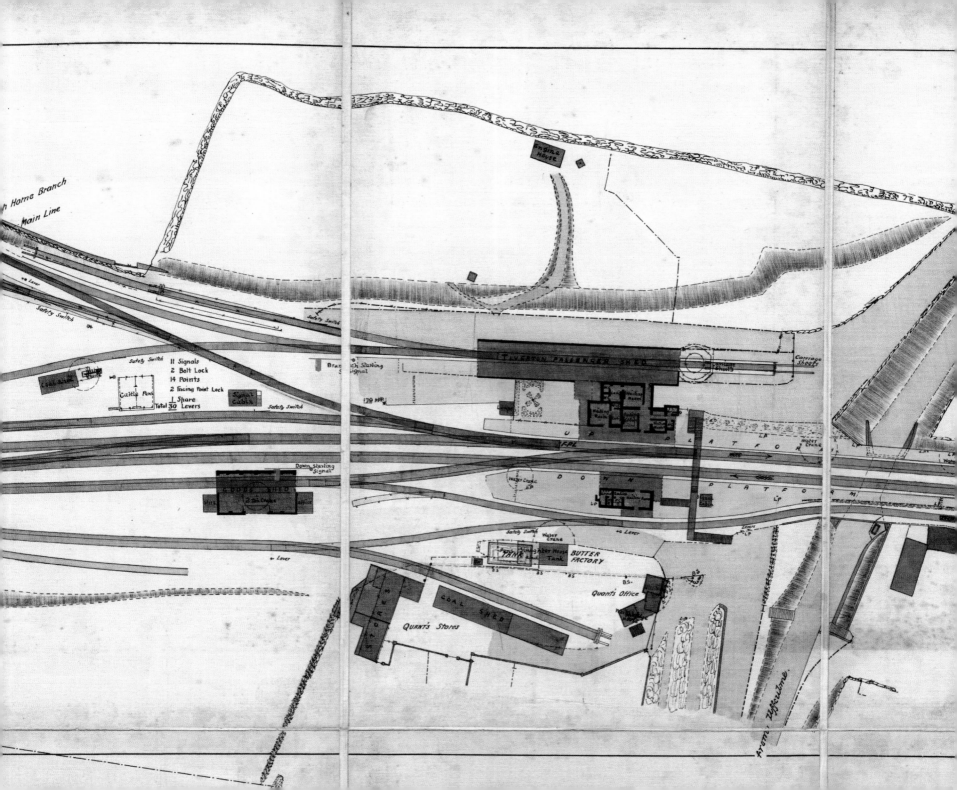

Home Branch

Main Line

Safety Switch

Safety Switch

11 Signals
2 Bolt Lock
14 Points
2 Facing Point Lock
1 Share
Total 30 Levers

Cattle Pens

COAL SHED

Safety Switch

Signal Cabin

Safety Switch

Branch Starting Signal

TIVERTON PASSENGER SHED

Carriage Sheds

Turntable

129 MR

U P   P L A T F O R M

F.P.L

Water Crane

Down Starting Signal

GOODS SHED

D O W N   P L A T F O R M

Hand Crane

Engine House

Safety Switch

Water Crane

TANK

Engine House and Tank

BUTTER FACTORY

Quant's Office

Quant's Stores

STORES

COAL SHED

Aram Thorndale.

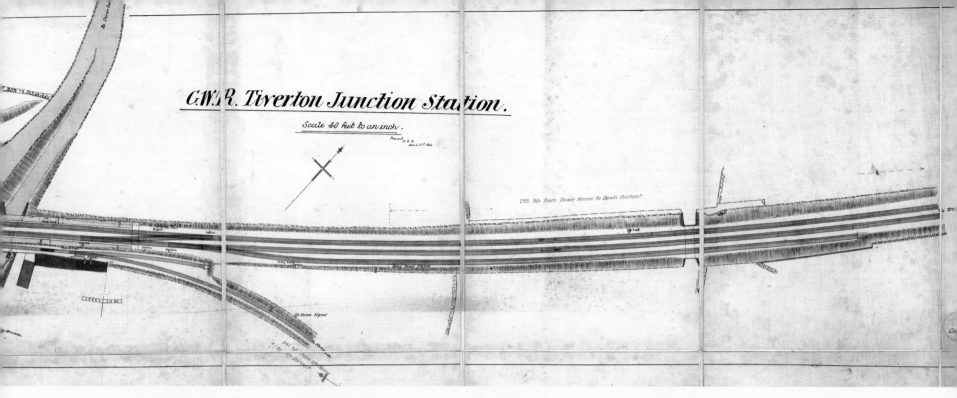

GWR. Tiverton Junction Station.

Scale 40 feet to an inch.

The main line Tiverton Junction Station in 1888 showing the mixed gauge main line and standard gauge branches.

Opened as Tiverton Road, the station was sited here as a result of a petition to the B & E Railway directors from the Tiverton Turnpike Trust. The alternative proposed site later became Sampford Peverell Halt and more recently Tiverton Parkway. The road through Sampford Peverell was felt to be too dangerous, particularly in view of the increased traffic that the railway would bring.

An interesting feature are the signals, encompassing both disc and crossbar examples and the more modern semaphore styles, the former on the two branch lines. Two types of junction signal are also apparent, the conventional bracket: as witness the home signals coming off the Tiverton Branch and the Branch signals for the Hemyock line, which have two arms on the same post.

The original signal cabin is opposite the goods shed and an additional one has been installed on the Down platform to control Culm Valley trains. Both branches show headshunts used to fly-shunt the stock and so enable locomotives to run round. As Culm Valley trains left the station, they immediately faced a climb at 1 in 66. The lightweight tank engines used prior to the introduction of the 48xx/14xx locos in the 1930s, meant that this climb could be a real obstacle particularly on heavier market day trains when several attempts were often needed! It is recorded that at least one Sunday School outing required passengers to get out and walk! Several abortive attempts at the climb could also require a return visit to the water column to ensure sufficient to reach Hemyock.

Of particular note are the station gardens on the Up platform. The Bristol & Exeter Railway started a competition for a best kept station master's garden and this idea was taken up by the GWR who provided a plant nursery in each division. The last, at Gloucester, closed in, circa 1936.

Most of what is seen here was swept away during rebuilding in the 1930s. Again the area is a mass of local industry with the various names and businesses worthy of careful study.

THE CULM VALLEY ROUTE

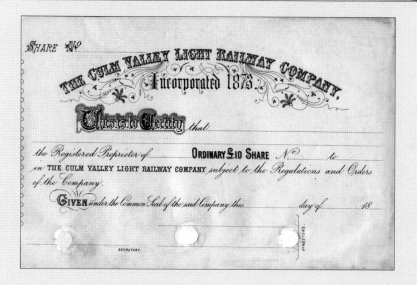

The picturesque, but far from financially viable, Culm Valley Railway had its origins in the minds of various landowners and farmers of the area.

Encouraged no doubt by the apparent success of the main Bristol and Exeter Railway, they sought to capitalise on the advantages of the railway age at the same time availing themselves of the benefits both of rail transport for their own goods and no doubt the belief of a worthwhile financial return on their investment.

In consequence, in 1873 an Act of Parliament was obtained for a Light Railway under a little used provision of the 1868 Regulation of Railways Act. (The specification for a Light Railway was intended to reduce the need for capital expenditure.)

At the time, the belief locally was that the 7 mile route could be completed for just £30,000 and ready for traffic by the end of 1874.

Both were destined to be woefully inaccurate. The eventual cost was £50,000 and the line did not open for traffic until 29 May 1876 (Oak Apple Day - a public holiday), whilst traffic generated and consequently receipts, were half that expected.

To be operated from the outset by the larger Bristol and Exeter concern, it must have come as a relief to the shareholders when just 4 years later in April 1880, the route was sold to the Great Western Railway, they in the meanwhile having absorbed the Bristol and Exeter line.

Unfortunately, so far as the investors were concerned, their £50,000 investment turned into a £17,000 loss, the GWR acquiring the route for just £33,000.

It was a story repeated in numerous locations throughout the country, a small independent concern unable to cope with the costs of operating a railway through sparse countryside and consequently sold, usually at a loss, to a larger company.

Thus was the way that the GWR became the mighty organisation it developed into. There was no place for sentiment in the boardroom at Paddington when dealing with the locals of Devon. The GWR had financial difficulties of their own at the time.

THE CULM VALLEY ROUTE

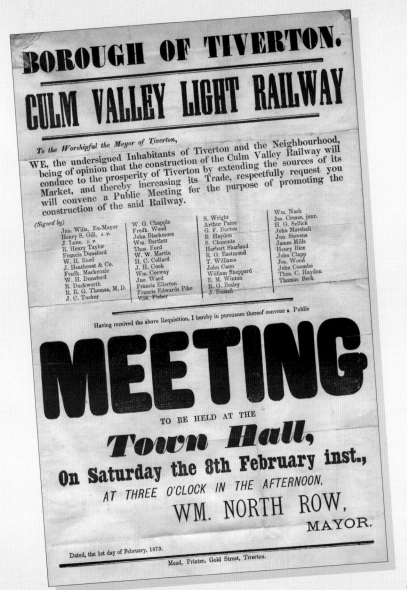

BOROUGH OF TIVERTON.

CULM VALLEY LIGHT RAILWAY

To the Worshipful the Mayor of Tiverton,

WE, the undersigned Inhabitants of Tiverton and the Neighbourhood, being of opinion that the construction of the Culm Valley Railway will conduce to the prosperity of Tiverton by extending the sources of its Market, and thereby increasing its Trade, respectfully request you will convene a Public Meeting for the purpose of promoting the construction of the said Railway.

(Signed by)

Jno. Wills, Ex-Mayor	W. G. Chapple	S. Wright	Wm. Nash
Henry S. Gill, J. P.	Fredk. Wood	Arthur Paine	Jas. Crease, junr.
J. Lane, J. P.	John Blackmore	G. F. Burton	H. G. Sellick
R. Henry Taylor	Wm. Bartlett	R Haydon	John Marshall
Francis Dunsford	Thos. Ford	S. Clements	Jno. Stevens
W. H. Reed	W. W. Martin	Herbert Sharland	James Mills
J. Heathcoat & Co.	H. C. Collard	R. G. Eastmond	Henry Rice
Fredk. Mackenzie	J. H. Cook	T. Williams	John Clapp
W. H. Dunsford	Wm. Cosway	John Cann	Jos. Wood
R. Duckworth	Jno. Ward	William Sheppard	John Coombe
R. R. G. Thomas, M. D.	Francis Ellerton	E. M. Winton	Thos. C. Haydon
J. C. Tucker	Francis Edwards Pike	R. G. Besley	Thomas Beck
	Vm. Fisher	J. Bussell	

Having received the above Requisition, I hereby in pursuance thereof convene a Public

MEETING

TO BE HELD AT THE

Town Hall,

On Saturday the 8th February inst.,

AT THREE O'CLOCK IN THE AFTERNOON,

WM. NORTH ROW,

MAYOR.

Dated, the 1st day of February, 1873.

Mead, Printer, Gold Street, Tiverton.

Above - Almost as an indication as to the perilous financial state of the little railway, some bills at least appear to have been prepared on ordinary paper.

Opposite page - The opening day at Hemyock, May 1876: hence the bunting. The goods shed is on the right. Aside from the great and the good, many of those present would no doubt have been investors too, their stern expressions to be repeated within just four years as their capital disappeared.

THE CULM VALLEY RAILWAY

THE CULM VALLEY RAILWAY

Top left - The change of date indicates the last minute delay in opening.

This page, right: No doubt in anticipation of goods times ahead, a celebratory luncheon was organised a few days after the opening. The numbers of those attending was not reported, whilst to be fair, this was also no more than was then standard practice when a railway opened. (Paid for by the Company no doubt!)

CULM VALE LIGHT RAILWAY

LUNCHEON, JUNE 1st, 1876.

MENU.

Boar's Head.

Galantines Veal.	Pressed Beef.
Hams.	Tongues.
Roast Beef.	Roast Pork.
Fillets Veal.	Raised Veal and Ham Pies.
Lamb.	Rounds Beef.
Pigeon Pies.	Roast Chicken.
Capons a la Bechamel.	Lobster Salads.

Noyeau Jellies.	Wine Jellies.
Chartreuse Jellies.	Russian Jellies.
Mille Fruit Cream.	Blanc Mange.
Gooseberry Tarts.	Open Tarts.
Fancy Pastry.	Rhubarb Tarts.

Ornamented Savoy Cakes.

DESSERT.

WINE LIST.

Champagne, qts. 7/- pts. 3/6 | Sherry qts. 5/- pts. 3/-
Claret, „ 5/- „ 2/6 | Sherry, „ 7/- „ 3/6
Port, qts. 6/- pts. 3/-

WITHERS & WRIGHT, COOKS AND CONFECTIONERS, CASTLE ST. AND MARTIN'S LANE, EXETER.

Chambers, Exeter.

Above - Hemyock showing the locomotive and carriage sheds. The refreshment room is to the right of the station. Note the ford through the river with access to the cattle pens via the gate.

Right - Hemyock Station and extract from the Tourist's Guide to North Devon. Not referred to is the Railway Hotel at Mill Hayes and a Refreshment Room in a field adjacent to the station.

Period travel guides recommended the walk to the Wellington Monument. It was hoped that visitor traffic could be developed sufficiently to justify building of another hotel near what became Whitehall Halt.

Railway Excursion.

XVI. TIVERTON JUNCTION TO HEMYOCK.

Distance from Tiv. Junc.	Station.	Distance from Hemyock.
2¾	Uffculme.	4¼
4¾	Culmstock.	2¼
7	Hemyock	

Time: 45m. *Fares:* (single) 1s. 6d., 1s., 8d., 7½d. (return) 2s. 3d., 1s. 6d. *Refreshments at inn at Junction.*

This little line is the parent "light railway" in the West of England. It embraces no heavy works of any kind, but simply runs up the valley of the Culm, keeping as near the surface level as possible, and following so closely the windings of the stream that again and again as the train glides along one may see the trout flitting hither and thither in the tree-shadowed waters. The scenery is pretty and pastoral for the most part, but becomes bolder near Hemyock, where the tract cuts across the flank of a spur of the Black Downs.

2¾m. UFFCULME. (Pop. 1811.) This thriving village, which boasts of a widely-known manufacture in the Uffculme ales, is very pleasantly situated right of the line. The ch. is a fine one, and includes examples of all the periods of Gothic architecture from E. Eng. to Perp. The tower is E. Eng., the body of the ch. chiefly Perp. Some of the arches are transitional in character, between E. Eng. and Dec. In this parish is Bradfield House, noted under Cullompton.

4¾m. CULMSTOCK. (Pop. 863.) There is nothing very noteworthy beyond the ch., which has a recent clerestory; while the lower stage of the tower is apparently Dec. The oddity here is that the tower has a thriving yew tree growing out of one of its sides. An ancient cope is preserved here.

7m. HEMYOCK. (Pop. 898.) A little place with no lack of attractions. For one thing, it nestles most pleasantly among the hills in what was, ere the railway whistle awoke the echoes, one of the most charming Sleepy Hollows of fair Devon. For a second, it is a capital centre for trout fishing. For a third, it has exceptional interest to the antiquary in its ch. and its castle. The *ch.* (rest.) is in the main Dec. It consists of chancel, nave, N. and S. aisles, W. tower, and an ancient sacristy N. of chancel. There are a couple of hagioscopes. The tower stands on E. Eng. arches to N., S., and E., as if it had been originally the central feature of a cruciform edifice. Other E. Eng. remains are found in some Purbeck columns in the vestry.

Hemyock Castle stands close by the ch. The main gateway and its towers remain, and the enclosing walls can still in great part be made out. It originally belonged to the ancient family of the Hidons, and the last warlike use it was put to was by the Roundheads, who made it do duty as a garrison and prison.

THE CULM VALLEY RAILWAY

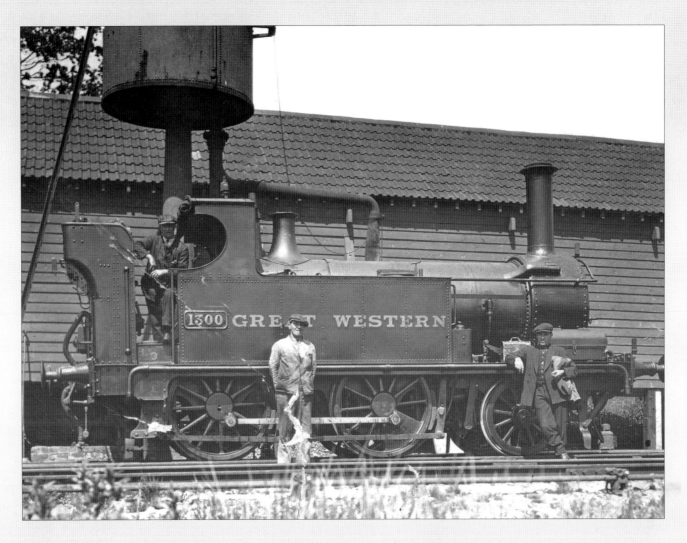

Former South Devon Railway, 2-4-0T No. 1300 in front of Hemyock carriage shed. Dating from December 1878, this along with sister engine No. 1298, was a regular performer on the branch throughout its life. It survived until May 1934. It was to enable replacement of these worn out, non-standard engines, that the branch was rebuilt and modernised, particularly the layout at Hemyock.

Amyas Crump collection

THE ARCHAEOLOGY OF THE RAILWAY

To the south of Bickleigh (later renamed Cadeleigh to avoid confusion with the station on the Tavistock branch), this bridge carries the main A396 road over the line. Today the trackbed forms the access road to the car park for the adjacent mill. The skew arch is of brick, still soot stained from passing trains, the last of which passed well over 40 years ago. Just out of camera to the left is a surviving ganger's hut, the main walls of which were once baulks in mixed gauge trackwork.

THE ARCHAEOLOGY OF THE RAILWAY

The first datum or bench mark shown on the diagram for the proposed Tiverton and North Devon Railway, was on the doorstep at the entrance to the Prince Blucher Public House in West Exe Street Tiverton - see page 6. The line north from here, as shown on page 6, was never built. Money was short and an alternative route, the 'Bolham Deviation' was approved and laid: at considerable saving in distance and expense.

Tiverton Goods Shed in Blundells Road. The original Bristol and Exeter building is at the far end. It had already been extended by the time the Tiverton and North Devon Railway was built - as can be seen in the background of the new station construction photographs.

The office extension on the right is of a later, standard GWR design. In recent years modern UPVC windows have been installed. The original glazing had overlapping panes.

THE ARCHAEOLOGY OF THE RAILWAY

The original, rather small, Goods Shed. The former rail entrance has now been blocked in, as at the time the view was taken, the site was due to be redeveloped. The dressed stone buttresses can be seen on the diagram on page 27.

The rendered section to the right would have been the original mid-way entrance for road vehicles. The office was behind the now blanked off window.

Both the original and the new stations have gone. However, the quality of materials used meant that when the later station was demolished, much of it was resold for salvage. Some is still to be seen in local gardens whilst certain buildings, such as the office of the Exe Valley Caravan Site at nearby Bridgetown, are readily recognisable.

The remains of the Gas Works in Blundells Road. The road level has been raised slightly, but the double wooden doors can be seen to extend below what is the present pavement level. It was at this point that a siding from the goods yard crossed the road at right angles before entering the gas works through these doors. Trucks would have been moved by horse or manpower as locomotives could not work over the numerous wagon turntables provided.

Above - Cove Crossing Signal Cabin and Keeper's Cottage, see page 15. The cottage has a recent rearward extension, enlarged porch and the chimney stack has been removed. Currently, similar buildings survive at Lodfin, Cadeleigh, Thorverton, Fortescue, and Brampford Speke.

Opposite page - Up Exe provides us with a good view of another similar building. In this case there has been a single storey extension of sympathetic design to the left. There is also a two storey rearward extension and the structure is also minus the original chimney stack. The ornate bargeboards survive on the porch.

THE ARCHAEOLOGY OF THE RAILWAY

THE ARCHAEOLOGY OF THE RAILWAY

THE ARCHAEOLOGY OF THE RAILWAY

Hemyock Engine Shed - built 1874.

One of the great pleasures of research is when the unexpected comes to light. Forty years ago I was told the Hemyock Engine Shed had been sold locally - this at the time it closed c1930. As it was an all-timber building dating from the mid 1870s, it was naturally assumed it had long disappeared. It was thus with considerable surprise that I was privileged to receive an invitation to visit this wonderful survivor. The profile clearly matches that illustrated on page 37. The doors are not original, these had been removed some time before closure, due, it was said, to avoid the structure being considered rateable.

The left side has recently been re-clad, internally some of the original survives (above left) and parts including the roof trusses (right), still display evidence of the original lime-wash. In its working life this unusual paint scheme had been applied on an annual basis, perhaps to reduce the risk of fire. When new, the shed cost £215 and the Carriage Shed £180. In 1930 both were rendered redundant following alterations to the line so as to permit the passage of larger engines. Both buildings were then included in an estimated £140 worth of recoverable materials.

THE ARCHAEOLOGY OF THE RAILWAY

Left - At Thorverton, the signal box went the way of so many wooden railway buildings. The goods shed too was demolished. The station having been sold for conversion to a private dwelling. Much of the booking office furniture was re-used by a local shop, but this has now closed so it has gone to Cadeleigh to assist in the restoration of that station.

How wondrous to be able to enjoy a garden where even the Cornish Riviera Express and at least two Royal Trains have passed. Like many rural stations, Thorverton was renowned for its floral displays, cuttings from which survive in several local gardens. The roses reportedly thrived as a result of the amount of tea drunk by the station staff and suitable gaps in the train service!

On Exeter Market Day, the adjacent water meadows were let out to local farmers to graze their horses. Going to market could be a thirsty business and horses could be relied upon to find their own way home!

In was in this village that Wm. Moss the contractor settled.

Opposite page - A boarded up Cadeleigh station, weighbridge office, goods shed, and bridge - see page 13. Now known as Devon Railway Centre, the station that time forgot. The bridge survives as it still carried mains services. For many years prior to the railway centre, the buildings lay empty, the site used by Devon County Council for storage of roadstone: and apparently litter bins. Notice the original barge boards on the station building.

THE ARCHAEOLOGY OF THE RAILWAY

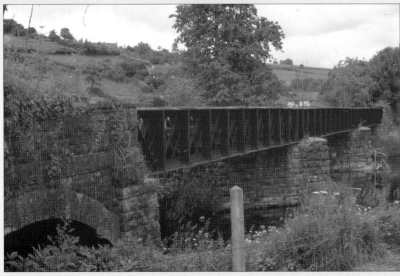

ACKNOWLEDGEMENTS

The origins of this book were inspired by looking through the Museum archives, therefore thanks for their support are due to: the staff and volunteers, particularly Judith Elsdon, Malcolm Kitchen, Roger Lambert and Liz Shepherd. Thanks are also due to Chris Henley, Glyn Jones and Alan Sainty for help with illustrations. Over many years my family, members of the Great Western Society, Thorverton History Society and the Broad Gauge Society, particularly Alan Garner and Geof Sheppard have also been very supportive, thanks also to Sean Bolan for permission to reproduce his beautiful painting on the cover, lastly to Kevin for believing in the project.

The Tiverton Museum of Mid Devon Life

Now celebrating its fiftieth year, this award winning collection housed in fifteen separate galleries includes examples of : Agricultural, Transport, Industry, Craft and Domestic life. The collection of farm vehicles is considered of national importance. The highly regarded Education department is the home of the website 'Virtual Victorians' used by schools across the world.

Tiverton Museum of Mid Devon Life
Buck's Square
TIVERTON
Devon
EX16 6PJ
01884 256295   Reg. Charity No. 239531

Opposite page - GWR 48xx (later BR 14xx) 0-4-2T No. 1442 in temporary outside preservation at Tiverton. This former branch locomotive now reposes within the Tiverton Museum.

The Broad Gauge Society

The Broad Gauge Society was formed in 1980 to promote research into and the modelling of the British 7ft 0¼in gauge railways of the 19th Century. It currently has over 300 members and meetings are held on a regular basis. Most Broad Gauge lines were built by the Great Western Railway and associated companies, many by the famous engineer Isambard Kingdom Brunel. The London & South Western and Midland Railways also owned and operated Broad Gauge lines for some years. The last Broad Gauge trains ran in May 1892.

The Society publishes a bi-monthly News-Sheet giving news of forthcoming meetings, new kits and other items of interest to members.

The Broadsheet is published twice a year on glossy art paper and contains articles on prototype and modelling subjects. Copies of back issues are available to new members.

A4 Data Sheets are published with most issues of the News-Sheet. There are now around 60 sheets in the New Series covering coaches and waggons plus 49 sheets in the Old Series covering permanent way. Members may purchase copies of these with new sheets being issued free to all members.

The Society also publishes A3 drawings and A4 data file sheets. The data file sheets include a wealth of hitherto unpublished material from the National Archive and elsewhere. There is also a sheet with recommended modelling standards.

Membership Cost

Membership costs £10.00 each year. New members will also need to pay a one-off £2.00 joining fee to cover the cost of a pack which includes much information on the broad gauge railways and where to find information and artefacts. Overseas members also pay £2.00 per year postage supplement (or £6.00 for airmail outside Europe).

Please contact the Membership Secretary (membership@broadgauge.org.uk) for all membership enquiries.